MW00630029

For Noah and Selah —
you will always be loved by me.

When your heart is heavy inside of your chest,
Or your day is hard and you feel a tad stressed,
When nothing goes right and everything seems wrong,
I will love you big and I will love you strong.

If you run super fast and make all your shots,
Or you stumble and fall but give it all you got...

No matter the outcome, no matter the score,
I will love you more and more.

You could drive a big truck or fly a small plane,
Become a skilled surgeon and operate on a brain,
Whatever you decide, whatever you choose,
Nothing could lessen how much I love you.

When you dance to the beat inside of your head,
When you want to be mean but choose kindness instead...

When you leap toward your dragons, with courage and might,
I'll be right beside you, joining in on your fight.

When you think you're invisible, forgotten, or unseen,
Or if someone says something that's hurtful and mean...

I want you to know that those things just aren't true —
The unshakeable fact is you're loved through and through.

I know you are brave, I know you are smart,
I know when you speak that you speak from your heart.

May you always have hope, even if that hope's small —
A hope that the world can be better for all.

You add color and light to a world that feels dark,
No matter what happens, hold tight to your spark.

You will always belong, despite how you may feel.
God and I both think you're a pretty big deal.

You are brighter than all of the stars in the sky,
More dazzling than fireworks shooting up high...

You were designed with a purpose, a great plan in mind,
You were made to be loved, you are one of a kind.

I pray you become a person of love,
And at the end of each day, you've done things you're proud of.

I pray people see God's pure love in you,
And know deep within that they're loved by Him too.

If there comes a day when you feel all alone,
You've gone far away and you want to come home,
Look inside your heart and then you will see...

Wherever you are — you're loved by me.